ANGLING FOR WORDS

BASIC ANGLING PRACTICE BOOK

Teacher's Manual

Revised Edition

Dorothy B. Montgomery
Linda M. Gipson

Decoding and Spelling Practice with Basic Vocabulary

Academic Therapy Publications
Novato, California

Academic Therapy Publications
20 Leveroni Court
Novato, California 94949-5746

19 18
13 12 11 10 09 08 07 06 05

ISBN: 0-87879-519-7
ISBN 13: 978-0-87879-519-2

FOREWORD

The *Basic Angling Practice Book* is the authors' attempt to add to the *Angling for Words* series an adaptation of *Angling's* decoding and spelling program which is designed especially for the primary, remedial, learning disabled, or adult illiterate student on the basic vocabulary level. Our thirty-five combined years of teaching decoding and spelling skills in resource room, remedial class, primary group, and individual therapy settings had convinced us of the need for a practical, economical practice book which could be used by volunteer tutors, aides, and parents as well as teachers.

The *Basic Angling Practice Book* was field tested by the authors during the three years of the development of its format. During the 1984-85 school year, the Field Test Edition was utilized by selected instructors serving in the following educational settings: regular first and second grade phonics groups, resource rooms, elementary remedial reading class, public school group tutoring program, rehabilitation center, elementary English as a Second Language class, programs for foreign-born and illiterate adults, private schools for learning disabled students, parent-child instruction, individual tutoring, and language therapy.

The field test instructors were unanimous in their enthusiasm for the flexibility and simplicity of the use of the book. The comments within their evaluations of it included:

> *"The format makes it so easy to use, I can't imagine working with my students without it."* (private tutor)

> *"It was valuable as a basic instructional tool as well as a very good supplemental program . . . It belongs in every resource room."* (LD-EMR resource teacher)

> *"A non-reading mother is being tutored by her child after we have read the word lists here. The choice of words is excellent and quite appropriate for the students."* (rehabilitation center therapist)

> *"I have found the book . . . of tremendous value in helping children who are . . . Spanish speakers."* (ESL teacher)

To all of the instructors, schools, institutions, and students who confirmed our faith in this book by testing it, we are extremely grateful. We could not have produced it without the warm support and counsel from Carolyn Bowen and John Arena.

We are particularly grateful to our families for their tolerance and support over the past three years. We could not have completed the book without help from all of them.

Dorothy B. Montgomery
Linda M. Gipson

ABOUT THE AUTHORS

Dorothy B. Montgomery, MEd, has been a language, remedial, and reading specialist for more than twenty years in Wichita Falls, Texas. Having received a BA degree from the University of Texas, she began her teacher training with certification as a language therapist in the class with Carolyn Bowen, author of *Angling for Words*, at the Language Training Unit of Texas Scottish Rite Hospital in Dallas, Texas. She taught privately as a therapist before receiving teacher certification and entering public school teaching. She is the author of Phono-Cards and The Teacher's Line in the Angling series, which provided teachers in both public and private settings with a guide for using the program.

She was certified in Language/Learning Disabilities and received a master's degree in secondary education from Midwestern State University. She served six years as a high school resource teacher after four years of teaching remedial English and reading. Her certification as a reading specialist was earned in a second master's program. In 1979 she returned to private services and formed a partnership entitled Educational Service Associates with her two teacher daughters, one of whom, Linda M. Gipson, is co-author of this book. At the present time she practices as an educational therapist, reading specialist, and educational consultant in curriculum.

Professional awards have included being named Teacher of the Year by the Wichita Falls Classroom Teachers and Wichita Falls LDA and the Outstanding Teacher by the area Council for Exceptional Children. She has made numerous presentations at conferences and in-service workshops. Recently she has been active in guiding the formation of the Wichita Adult Literacy Council. Her professional activities also include Texas LDA, in which she served on the Professional Advisory Committee, Association of Educational Therapists, Delta Kappa Gamma, and the Orton Society.

Linda M. Gipson, MEd, received her BS degree in special education from the University of Houston and her master's degree from Midwestern State University, Wichita Falls, Texas. She earned four special education certifications and taught five years in Spring Branch and Wichita Falls schools as an elementary resource teacher before joining Educational Service Associates. Linda practices as a registered educational diagnostician, an educational therapist, and a curriculum consultant, with specialization in mathematics and reading.

She served as a consultant in the development of Project Guide II and Region IX Educational Service Center, Wichita Falls, Texas, and has given in-service and conference presentations on math disabilities. Awards include being named Elementary L/LD Resource Teacher of the Year by the Wichita Falls LDA for 1978-79 and to Outstanding Young Women of America. Her professional activities include LDA and Delta Kappa Gamma.

TABLE OF CONTENTS

INTRODUCTION

What are the uses of the *Basic Angling Practice Book*?

1. As a sequentially controlled program to develop basic skills in phonetic decoding and spelling.
   a. It may be supplemented, when student needs dictate, by a number of existing linguistic or multisensory materials compatible in sequence.
   b. As a program, it is most effective when used with the *Angling for Words Phono-Cards*.
   c. *The Teacher's Line* for *Angling for Words* provides detailed techniques and background for its use with students with mild Specific Language Disabilities.

2. As a structured presentation of phonics or supplementary practice material to strengthen a basal reading or linguistic reading program in primary grades.

3. As additional practice material for a phonics program or language therapy program already being used.

4. As a separate program of instruction in phonetic spelling to develop skill in spelling the large percentage of English words which are phonetically regular.

5. As a teacher's resource book of phonetically regular words and sentences for dictation and practice. Lists of non-phonetic basic and functional words are also provided as material for mastery in reading and spelling.

The *Basic Angling Practice Book* is not designed as

1. A separate beginning reading program for first grade or beginning reading classes since it is limited to decoding training. It has proven very effective, however, as an alternative type of instruction for children who have not been successful in learning to read well in a basal or sight word program.

2. A full language therapy program needed by specific dyslexics or by students with severe reading disabilities. *Basic Angling* can serve as a *part* of a multisensory program designed for such students.

For what instructional settings is the *Basic Angling Practice Book* designed?

This material is appropriate for small group or individual instruction in:

1. A regular first or second grade classroom.

2. A special education class for students with learning disabilities, mild dyslexia, mild visual handicaps, or EMR ability level.

3. A remedial reading or basic reading/spelling skills class.

4. A Chapter I or compensatory education class.

5. An after-school tutoring program.

6. An ESL (English as a Second Language) class or tutoring.

7. An Adult Education class or tutoring.

8. An Adult Literacy volunteer tutoring program.

What type of instructor can use *Basic Angling*?

It is designed to be used successfully by:

1. Classroom teachers, including those with limited background training in phonics.

2. Special education teachers, who might also wish to incorporate instructional techniques detailed in the accompanying *The Teacher's Line* manual for cases of reading disabilities or perceptual handicaps.

3. Educational therapists, clinics, or private tutors with the background and needs listed in (2) above.

4. Classroom instructional aides or volunteer parent tutors without special training in reading instruction.

5. Volunteer tutors in adult literacy programs.

6. Parents desiring to give their children additional instruction in phonics.

Instructions for the use of *Basic Angling* have deliberately been written in non-technical language to facilitate its use by instructors with limited training in education.

What distinctive features make the *Basic Angling Practice Book* effective for use on a basic level?

Benefits for the student:

1. Format features large type, wide spacing, and numbered sections for ease in keeping the place.

2. Control of the phonetic sequence insures continuous success for the student. No word is ever encountered in the sequence before adequate instruction to

read it has been provided.

3. Most words used are selected from a basic vocabulary.

4. Nonphonetic words are carefully limited to a small number of low-level Dolch or functional words.

5. The continuous review built into *Basic Angling* leads to mastery learning of decoding skills.

6. Sentence content is meaningful and appropriate to both young students and adults with basic vocabularies.

Benefits for the instructor:

1. The teacher's edition incorporates the entire student text with instructions for each page. An Appendix includes a phonetic survey for pre- or post-testing, a sample lesson plan, progress charts to display mastered phonograms in reading and in spelling for student and teacher reference, and listings of supplementary basic words and materials compatible in phonogram sequence with *Basic Angling*.

2. The spelling sequence is charted in the Appendix and built into the curriculum to permit its use with the reading program, as a separate program, or as supplementary material.

3. The format is designed to allow the instructor maximum flexibility in meeting individual student needs. Lists of practice words may be read horizontally or vertically for varied purposes. Words similar in structure are grouped by numbered sections on the page for instructor's choice. The phonetic controls permit use of several levels of instruction simultaneously without confusion.

4. The *Basic Angling Practice Book* allows an instructor without prior training in phonetic decoding or spelling to develop in students the manual skills level of decoding, which must be mastered before higher reading skills are achieved. The teacher can be confident that the book provides a linguistically sound curriculum for instruction.

TEACHING WITH *BASIC ANGLING*

Setting the Stage to Use *Basic Angling* as a Program

1. Determine the size of the group to be instructed, with a maximum of eight students recommended. One-to-one instruction is ideal but certainly not essential.

2. This instruction demands full instructor attention and interaction during the 20 to 30 minutes recommended for its use. Daily instruction is preferable, but three 30-45 minute lessons per week can also prove effective.

    Since most of the instruction with *Basic Angling* involves oral practice by the students, the group must be positioned to avoid distracting other students.

3. Determine if phonetic spelling will be taught with the reading training. The simultaneous teaching of spelling correlated with reading instills in the student a real understanding of the nature of English language patterns, which strengthens both reading and spelling. If time does not permit daily use of spelling, the use of it several times a week is recommended.

4. Determine if the *Angling Phono-Cards* will be used. Use of the green reading cards gives the students multisensory input, and the responses to the letters become automatic. Students with difficulties in learning sight words or phonics particularly need this daily practice.

    The pink *Phono-Cards* are designed for the teacher to give the sound and the students to respond with letter spellings. Both sets of cards are used for the lesson.

    If the *Phono-Cards* are not used, a chalkboard, felt-board, or other letter cards should be used with children with reading difficulties.

5. Each student should have a copy of the *Basic Angling Practice Book* for use during the class. The instructor needs the Teacher's Manual. Any available supplementary materials which are compatible in sequence will give added reinforcement and practice. (See page T 23 for a listing of these.) A chalkboard is also useful at times.

    In teaching students with known learning disabilities, the teacher will find *The Teacher's Line* and *Angling for Words* useful for detailed techniques and background. The chart for Spelling Curriculum, page T 32, gives the pages in *Teacher's Line* covering each phonogram.

Preparing for the First Lesson

1. If conditions permit individual survey testing and the student is above first grade placement:

   a. Copy the recording sheets of the *"Basic Angling* Phonetic Skills Survey" found on pages T 25.

   b. Read carefully the accompanying instructions and practice the correct sounds noted in the key to speed recognition of the correct response.

   Check the sound spellings in parentheses on the Spelling Curriculum Chart on page T 32 for the ways to mark errors made by the student.

   c. The student's copy to read is found on the first two pages of the *Basic Angling Practice Book.*

   d. The instructor may choose to administer just LEVEL Ia or only the first page as a pre-test instead of completing the entire survey before teaching begins. Remaining sections may be used as pre-tests later.

   e. The nonsense words in this survey may seem threatening to some students. The survey provides valuable information about the student's knowledge of phonics, but it should not be used if it makes a lower level student feel uncomfortable.

2. Using page T 30, copy the blank Trophy Chart on which the phonograms are to be recorded as they are mastered.

   a. One copy of the chart may be maintained and posted for a group, or individual copies may be kept. The completed chart on page T 31 is the key.

   b. Recording begins in the left square of the bottom row and proceeds to the right and then to the line above on left, as the instructions describe. This chart has proven very motivating to most students as they can see evidence of their progress.

3. Sort out the reading *Phono-Cards* needed.

   a. Select the green pre-entry consonant cards for t, p, n, s, l, d, f, h, g, m, r, c, k, b, j, v. Secure the cards with a rubber band.

   b. Have the yellow a card ready.

   c. Write the word "a" on a card or chalkboard to check if students can read it.

4. If spelling is to be included in the instruction, prepare the materials.

   a. Copy the Spelling Record sheet on page T 35.

   b. Sort out the pink spelling *Phono-Cards* for the letters which are to be taught for reading.

    c. Practice making the sounds in parentheses. The word at the bottom right is the key to the correct sound.

5. Look carefully at the format of the *Practice Book* before beginning instruction and note these features:

    a. The columns of short words are arranged so that each student in a group can read horizontally one or more rows. If a group has assigned seats and a different student begins each lesson, the practice words will be new to each student when the page is repeated.

    b. Use of a marker card below the line being read is helpful to many students in keeping the place.

    c. Reading words horizontally is usually easier practice and often involves only changing the initial consonant. Reading words vertically gives practice in mixed words. Words are usually more difficult toward the bottom of the page. Choose direction and sections practiced according to needs.

    d. "Words" listed below the *** on any page, as in item 5 of page one, are nonsense syllables and are consequently perfectly phonetic for reading and spelling. Nonsense syllables and words are used on a few early pages to test whether the student can use the phonograms on unfamiliar short "words."

    e. Except for the limited number of Learned Words which must be taught to the students for reading and spelling, all words used in *Basic Angling* are phonetically regular for *reading*. Words not regular for *spelling* are found in the far right column of each page and should not be dictated.

    f. Phrases and sentences are best read aloud by the student after they have been read silently in preparation. This develops fluency and comprehension.

    g. The introduction of phonograms is controlled so that different subsections of some levels are correlated, and abler students can progress more rapidly. These options will be described as they are encountered.

Beginning the Instruction with *Basic Angling*

1. Determine the knowledge of letter sounds the students have as the instruction begins.

    a. Administer the *"Basic Angling* Phonetic Skills Survey" to individuals when possible and appropriate. Follow instructions in the Appendix, pages T 25-T 26.

    b. Using the *Phono-Cards* or written letters, check the students' mastery of the pre-entry phonograms. These consonants are (in the approximate order they are found in the green *Phono-Cards*):

        t, p, n, s (s), l, d, f, h,
        g (g), m, r, c (k), b, j, v

The student should be able to give the sound for each letter. A word using the correct sound is listed for the instructor on the back of each *Phono-Card*.

If the student gives (z) for s̲, (s) for c̲, or (j) for g, ask for the more common other sound the letter has. Do not, during this check, correct the student for making excessive "uh" sound at the end of any responses. Make that correction in the next lesson.

Any of these consonant sounds which have not already been mastered must be learned before beginning in the *Basic Angling Practice Book*. They may be taught by readiness phonics workbooks, techniques described in *The Teacher's Line*, page 27, or by the instructor's chosen methods.

Check to make sure the student can read the word "a."

c. Check to see if the student knows:

(1.) The alphabet. He should be able to say it and write it either in manuscript or cursive. Can he write capital and lower case forms? Note.

(2.) The names of the vowels? (a̲, e̲, i̲, o̲, u̲, y̲) Did he add "And sometimes y̲?" Note answers. Does he know which letters are consonants? (All those which are not vowels. Y̲ is both.)

(3.) The concept of a syllable. See page T 8, item e̲ for background on which to base judgment of students' understanding of syllables.

d. Teach any unmastered skills or concepts in (c) above within the first few weeks as opportunity arises.

2. Begin the instruction, taking care to reassure the students that they will be able to learn this way.

a. Tell the students that, even though they probably know other letters and sounds, this program will never ask them to read anything that has not been covered in *this* instruction. They should remember to use *only* what will be introduced here.

b. Review the consonants checked in (1) (b) above:

(1.) Show the consonant *Phono-Cards* one at a time to the students for their response with the correct sound. Correct (with gentleness) unnecessary "uh" sounds given at the end of the consonants.

(2.) It is best for the student to learn and respond with the key word listed and then the sound he has just heard in the word. Other key words previously learned or the instructor's choices may be submitted. Some students already know the consonant sounds well and may be permitted to respond with just the sound if it is accurate. Vowels are more difficult and use of key words is advised.

(3.) Record, or ask the students to record, on the Trophy Chart the consonant phonograms checked and given correctly. (Use other key, page T 31.)

c. Introduce the short sound of vowel <u>a</u> with the yellow vowel card.

   (1.) Name the letter, say the key word, "apple," and the sound (ă) clearly. Students repeat.

   (2.) Explain that this is the short sound of <u>a</u> and that it makes this sound when it is closed by one or more consonants following it. Use the *Phono-Cards* to demonstrate with the word "at." Remove the <u>t</u> and read the word "a," in which the <u>a</u> has the long sound because it is open.

   This is an important concept for the student to understand – that his eyes can tell him the sound of a vowel by seeing what follows it. Repeat this teaching whenever necessary until the student thoroughly understands it.

   (3.) Record the short <u>a</u> on the Trophy Chart, second row, first square on the left.

d. On the desk or in a card display, make words with cards using one consonant, the <u>a</u>, and a closing consonant. Do not use <u>h</u>, or <u>r</u> as the final consonant. Observe if the students are able to recognize or blend these short <u>a</u> words.

   If they are unable to blend the sounds, more preparation must be made before beginning the *Practice Book*. See the techniques in *The Teacher's Line*, page 27, or other introductory level manuals.

e. Explain the concept of a syllable with these facts:

   (1.) A syllable must have and only can have one vowel sound. The word "I" is a syllable, "ran" is one syllable, and "rain" is one syllable because two vowels only make one sound. The word "name" is one syllable because the final <u>e</u> is not pronounced.

   (2.) Syllables in longer words will usually follow the phonetic patterns which *Basic Angling* teaches. There are only a few patterns of syllable division used in English. Therefore, if the student learns the regular phonograms and the patterns of syllable division taught in this book, he should be able to read a large majority of English words.

   Levels Ia and Ib of *Basic Angling* contain only words of one closed syllable with the short vowel sound so that the student can internalize a basic structure of the English language.

f. Have the students read in turn as many of the words on page 1 as time and circumstances permit. In this program, all words must be read exactly as written; "a" cannot be read "the."

   When a student makes an error, calmly say something like, "Is it?" or "Look at that again." Be supportive with positive comments whenever possible.

g. Explain to the students that the nonsense syllables could well be parts of longer real words, as "han" in "handle," "fam" in "family," and "bap" in "Baptist."

3. After reading page 1, tell the students that they will now see how they can spell the same words they have been reading without studying the spelling.

   a. Using the pink *Phono-Cards*, the instructor gives the sounds for the phonograms introduced for reading.

   b. The students repeat the sound and give the name of the letter which spells that sound as they write the letter. Continue through all phonograms introduced.

   c. Note that there are two spellings for the sound (k): c and k. The student should give and write both. It is at this point that the instructor should teach that English uses c whenever it can at the beginning of a word. As the card states, k is the spelling before e, i, or y. This is true because c has the (s) sound before those three letters (but the students do not know this yet).

      Do not use the second spellings listed for other letters until they are added in the spelling curriculum. The teacher instructions will tell you when to add.

   d. Record the spellings just given on the spelling chart copied from page T 35. Also record the date of this lesson by the "(k) Initial" on the first line below.

   e. Dictate selected words from the first three columns on page one. Include "cap" to test the use of c as introduced. Eight to ten words are usually enough.

      The students should repeat the word dictated and then say the letters softly aloud as they write them. If this is disturbing, have them move their lips saying the letter names to themselves. This gives some additional feedback to the student.

      It is very important to have each student then read back to himself what he has actually written. This practice reinforces the reading instruction and instills the necessary skill of proofreading. Allow corrections. Take up the papers to check mastery.

4. This ends the first lesson. Review how the students did on each aspect of the lesson before making the next lesson plan.

What is included in the lesson plan for each session?

1. Each lesson should have the following parts, preferably in the order listed:

   a. Student responses to all *Phono-Cards* covered to date. These should be shuffled before each use and are easily kept separate by a rubber band.

   b. Review practice of the past few phonograms covered through practice in the *Basic Angling* pages dealing with each. The entire page is not usually done; select numbered sections, horizontal or vertical practice, and variety in the words assigned.

   c. Introduction of a new phonogram or concept when students show some mastery of the phonograms covered to date. Add the card to deck and list on chart.

d. Practice on the new phonogram from page in *Basic Angling*.

e. Practice in a supplemental material if available. (See page T 23.) Be sure to check the phonogram controls and sight words used in other materials. The student should not be given material containing any phonograms or sight words not yet covered in this instruction. If only a few Learned Words are present, these could be taught before reading.

Practice in supplemental story books with identical controls does help build fluency in reading.

f. Spelling sounds from *Phono-Cards* pack and dictation of words and sentences from pages which have been covered in *Basic Angling*. If time does not permit this instruction at each lesson, schedule it every few lessons.

In choosing words or sentences for spelling dictation, be sure to include review phonograms and generalizations and spellings which are causing the students particular difficulty.

2. A blank sample lesson plan form and an actual lesson plan which might be used after several weeks of instruction are included on page T 29.

What else do I need to know as I teach with *Basic Angling*?

1. The following pages of the Teacher's Manual, before the student's *Basic Angling Practice Book* begins, are page by page notations of any pertinent information needed for either reading or spelling instruction.

2. Since *The Teacher's Line* contains more detailed background explanation, the pages from that manual which deal with a phonogram or concept will be noted in the instructions as applicable. They will be marked T.L. with the related page number.

3. Pages in the *Angling for Words Study Book* which have identical controls will be noted in these instructions.

INSTRUCTIONAL COMMENTARY

LEVEL Ia – Short vowels, one syllable, single consonant sounds

Page 1 – Follow instructions given in detail in pages T 5 through T 10 for the first lesson using page 1.

Note that the first sections change only the initial consonant when read horizontally. Reading vertically requires more mastery of the consonant sounds.

Remember that the nonsense syllables could be parts of real English words.

Any words which are irregular for spelling are found in the far right column, so avoid dictating these.

For students who displayed ability to blend consonants in the *Phonic Survey* or show some ability to blend easily, proceed to page 14 and try the students on the short a blends. If they are able to blend, LEVEL Ib pages can be used simultaneously to speed instruction.

Page 2 – Introduce short i for reading and spelling. Techniques in *The Teacher's Line*, (T.L. p. 27), should be used with severe disabilities. Add card and list on Trophy Chart.

Section #3 is designed to be read vertically from the left column to the right column since this employs "minimal differences" practice, (one letter is changed in each successive word). This develops discrimination of the consonant changes.

Page 15 introduces short i blends and can be used now with the stronger student if desired. See page T 13.

Page 3 – Mixed vowel practice develops discrimination. The pairs in each section are read vertically for this purpose. Reading horizontally provides mixed words.

Techniques for spelling dictation are to be found in T.L., page 28.

Page 4 – Introduce the voiced sound of s (z) and the concept of a plural being a *spelling* to show more than one. The (s) endings in #2 follow particular consonants. The voice usually takes care of producing the correct sound for final s̲ without the speaker's conscious thought. Response to s̲ reading card becomes (s), (z).

The s̲ is the regular spelling for (z) except at the beginnings of words. Give only the s̲ response now.

Page 5 – Introduce short u̲ for reading and spelling. The format of the page remains the same.

Pages 16 and 17 include short u̲ blends and more difficult sentences for the stronger student's use now.

Page 6 – Final double consonants usually present no problem for reading since the consonant is just sounded once.

Teach the spelling generalization from T.L., p. 38, that final (f), (l), and (s) in one-syllable words, immediately following a short vowel sound, are usually spelled ff, ll, ss. Common explanations are us̲, bus̲, gas̲, plus̲, yes̲, if̲, and pal̲. Teach these.

Page 7 – Introduce short e̲ for reading and spelling. Many students have difficulty hearing the difference between short i̲ and e̲, especially before n̲ and m̲. Sections #3 and #4 are to be read vertically.

Page 18 has short e̲ blends for the able student.

Page 8 – The discrimination practice includes the vowels covered; groups are read vertically to test ability to produce the correct vowel sound. Section #4 is mixed.

Introduce w̲ for reading and spelling. T.L., p. 51.

Page 9 – Teach the Learned Words before assigning the sentences. The̲, go̲, and he̲ are phonetically regular but the concept of open long vowels is not taught until LEVEL IIa, p. 49. Techniques for teaching sight words for reading and spelling are found on page 29 in T.L.

Introduce initial consonant y̲ (y) for reading and spelling. T.L., pp. 42-3, has background information on y̲.

Page 10 – Introduce short o̲ for reading and spelling. Included here are some basic words in which the short o̲ sound is not pure: dog̲, log̲, off̲, on̲. The basic level student can usually read these familiar words without awareness of a sound difference. Similar words are toss̲, loss̲, lost̲, soft̲, floss̲ on p. 19, and song̲ and long̲ on p. 24.

Page 11 – Introduce final x̲ (ks), which is difficult to say in isolation. T.L., pp. 52-3. For spelling, x̲ is regular for (ks). Continue to add cards introduced and to chart.

Introduce z̲ (z) for reading. For spelling, z̲ is the second response now added for (z) but is regular only at the beginning of a base word. See T.L., p. 52. Double z̲ is a common ending, but zz words must be learned. Add Learned Words i̲ and you̲ for reading and spelling.

Pages 12-13 – Minimal differences for vertical practice and mixed sentences for review.

LEVEL Ib – Short vowels, consonant blends, consonant digraphs

Pages 14-22 – Short vowels with consonant blends. Short sections on these practice pages contain pairs to be read vertically, adding a consonant to make a blend. Advanced practice in the *Angling Study Book*, pp. 4-16, 21, 33.

Pages 20-21 – Practice in changing initial blends or consonants when read horizontally. Vertical practice is in changing the short vowel sound. Section #4 on p. 20 changes the vowel sound horizontally and the second consonant of the blend when read vertically.

Page 23 – Add final <u>ck</u> (k), regularly found at the end of one syllable words directly following a short vowel sound.

Add the spelling generalization for final (k) in one syllable words: Use <u>k</u> after a consonant and <u>ck</u> after a short vowel. <u>T.L.</u>, p. 47. Practice in the *Angling for Words Workbook* for this is found on pp. 12-14.

Add Learned Words <u>there</u>, <u>come</u>, and <u>are</u> for reading and spelling.

Page 24 – Add <u>nk</u> and <u>ng</u> for reading and spelling, although they are often best added at different lessons to avoid confusion. Note the difference in tongue position between (n) and (ngk) if the students have trouble saying the blends in isolation.

Page 25 – Add <u>sh</u> for reading and spelling.

Page 26 – Add both the voiced and unvoiced sounds of <u>th</u>. There are obviously more of the (th) words; the second pronunciation is found most often in these familiar words. Teach <u>this</u> and <u>thus</u> as exceptions to the <u>ss</u> spelling.

Page 27 – Add <u>ch</u> (ch) for reading. The (k) and (sh) sounds for <u>ch</u> are not usually taught at the basic skills level. Common words like <u>school</u> and <u>Christmas</u> are learned as sight words when needed. See <u>T.L.</u>, page 72.

Add <u>tch</u> (ch) for reading following a short vowel; the <u>t</u> is not pronounced and is from Old English spelling.

Teach the (ch) spelling generalization here if the students are mature enough for it. See <u>T.L.</u>, pp. 72-3. <u>Ch</u> is the regular spelling except at the end of a one syllable word after a short vowel when <u>tch</u> is used.

Exceptions to the (ch) spelling generalization should be taught in the common words <u>much</u>, <u>such</u>, and <u>rich</u>.

Page 28 – Add <u>wh</u> for reading and spelling. The sound is made by blowing out air (hw). Teach <u>which</u> for spelling.

Add <u>qu</u> (kw), regular for reading and spelling in base words. The letter <u>q</u> is rarely used in English words without the <u>u</u>; <u>u</u> is not considered a vowel in this combination and is treated as a <u>w</u>. <u>T.L.</u>, pp. 53-54.

LEVEL Ic – Short vowel words with suffixes; -C(onsonant)<u>le</u> words, compound words, and VC/CV and VCCCV words.

This section may be postponed for first grade students or those not ready for two-syllable words. Proceed to LEVELS II and III in those cases. However, some students might attempt the compound words on pages 40-41 now.

Page 29 — Short vowel base words with the suffix -ing added. This practice develops the perceptual ability to focus on the base word and then add the familiar suffix.

Sections #3 and #4 involve reading base words where the final consonant has been doubled. Although this pattern is actually the VC/CV not yet taught, it has been found that most students will attack these words as the ones in #1 and #2 since the double letter is only pronounced once. If there is difficulty, delay these sections until later in the LEVEL.

The spelling rule for doubling the final consonant of a CVC word when a suffix beginning with a vowel is added is logically taught here. Page 111 of T.L. has explanation, as do most spelling manuals. If this rule is not taught here, do not dictate words or sentences containing the doubled consonant before a suffix.

Page 30 — The vowel y (ĭ) is difficult for many students and is introduced here in its most common position, as a suffix on the end of a base word or doubled consonant.

Teach that the vowel y is another spelling for i, and that English words do not regularly end in i but use y instead. The unaccented final y usually has the short i sound, but many students and some texts will use a long e sound for it. Use teacher judgment on whether to try to change this pronunciation. Recognition of the i - y relationship does not help spelling, since y is the regular spelling for final short i. T.L., p. 43.

Add the *Phono-Card* for vowel y (yellow) here, but only give the "candy (ĭ)" response at this point.

Page 31 — Suffix -ly is placed on base words without changing their spelling. Add Mr., Mrs., and said for both reading and spelling. Discuss abbreviations here.

Page 32 — The suffix ed is added to base words and has one of three sounds, depending upon the final letter of the base word. The ed is a separate syllable (ĕd) after a final t or d. This is an important visual clue.

Page 33 — Here the ed has the (t) sound after such final sounds as (k), (p), and (s). Add ed as the second spelling response for (t).

Page 34 — Add the (d) response along with the (t) for ed now. Add ed as the second spelling response for (d).

In reading words ending in the ed suffix, the voice will usually respond naturally with (t) or (d). Teach that in unfamiliar words the ed is pronounced (ĕd) only after a t or d except for a few exceptions like "crooked" or poetic words. T.L., pp. 49-50.

T 14

Page 35 – The suffix <u>er</u> is added to base words. Add the *Phono-Cards* for <u>er</u> for reading and spelling. The concept of the meaning of a suffix is here introduced. Teach this by going through the list, saying, "A helper is a person who helps;" "a mixer is a thing which mixes." The <u>er</u> "more" suffix is added when two things are compared.

Page 36 – Add the Learned Words <u>here</u>, <u>look</u>, and <u>was</u> for reading and spelling.

It is optional for the instructor to teach the concepts of contractions and possessives here. The words become regular for reading by ignoring the apostrophe. For spelling, the student must understand that the apostrophe replaces omitted letters in a contraction and is used with <u>s</u> in a possessive. Do not dictate these unless this is taught.

Page 37 – The suffix <u>es</u> (ĕz) is pronounced as a separate syllable on a base word ending in <u>s</u>, <u>x</u>, <u>z</u>, <u>ch</u>, or <u>sh</u>. This suffix can be heard and is spelled regularly.

Pages 38-39 – The final syllable -<u>ble</u>, -<u>dle</u>, etc. is an exception to the rule that every syllable must have a vowel sound, since the final <u>e</u> is silent. This syllable is never accented; instead, the syllable immediately preceding it gets the accent. The syllable is divided immediately in front of the -C(onsonant)<u>le</u>, a division which on these pages forms a closed syllable that consequently has a short vowel sound. See <u>T.L.</u>, p. 100.

The -C(onsonant)<u>le</u> pattern is regular for spelling. The dropped <u>e</u> plus <u>ed</u> rule may be taught here. <u>T.L.</u>, p. 110.

Pages 40-41 – Compound words with short vowels give practice in developing the perceptual ability to see the division between the two words. These words may be dictated.

Pages 42-44 – The common division of syllables with a vowel-consonant-consonant-vowel pattern is between the two consonants. Remind the students that a syllable must have and can only have one vowel sound. Page 42 leaves space between the syllables to help the student perceive the division. The second syllable often has an (ŭ) sound for its unaccented vowel; most students learn quickly to give an unaccented sound from having heard the words, so it is usually not necessary to teach this.

The words in each section on page 43 match those in the same section of page 42 but are not separated and are in a different order. Students can usually progress fairly quickly to being able to divide with their eyes. In case of difficulty, page 43 can be copied, and the students can draw vertical lines to divide syllables.

Teach that syllables are usually spelled exactly as they sound. In dictating VCCV words, stress each syllable. When only one consonant sound is heard after a short vowel, the consonant is regularly doubled, as in <u>rabbit</u>. Teach and put on Spelling Chart. <u>T.L.</u>, p. 54.

Page 45 – Here the VCCV words end in <u>y</u> which is short. There are only a few two-syllable words ending in the unaccented long <u>i</u> sound. The words in

Section #3 have the accent on the second syllable. See if the students can hear and produce the difference in accent. An accented closed syllable will have the pure short sound.

Pages 46, 48 – Review practice sentences.

Page 47 – Three consonants between two vowels usually do not pose much difficulty for reading or spelling since the voice will usually divide between the single consonant and consonant blend. It can be tried both ways if the division does not come naturally.

The vowel before two r's followed by a vowel is regularly short and does not form the vowel-r special sounds found in LEVEL IV. Introduce this pattern for reading and spelling. Many students mispronounce this pattern because they have not been taught that their eyes signal them to respond with a short vowel before two r's. These words are classed as "rabbit" words for spelling. T.L., pp. 41-2. *Angling Study Book* practice on pp. 16-22.

LEVEL IIa – Single long vowel situations; soft c (s)

Page 49 – Teach that in English one-syllable, one-vowel words, a final open vowel has the long sound and "says its name" (except for y). Add the long sound as the second response to the vowel reading cards and the first response in spelling long vowels. Review that it is the consonant closing a vowel that gives it the short sound. Read #2, #3, and #4 vertically to reinforce this concept.

Add the long sound of y (i) as a response to the card for vowel y. The y is long because it is open and accented. Add y as the regular spelling for (i) only at the end of a word, placing it in the third (i) space.

LEVEL IIb – Long vowel-consonant-silent e pattern.

Pages 50 - 53 – Add in order the a-C-e, i-C-e, and o-C-e. The student learns to respond to the visual pattern of letters with the long vowel sound. Practice is given also in discriminating between the short closed vowel pattern and the V-C-e. These pairs are read vertically.

Add a-C-e, i-C-e, and o-C-e as regular for spelling a long vowel sound followed by a single consonant sound. Long vowel digraph spellings will be found in LEVEL III to be regular for reading but must be learned for spelling since the V-C-e spelling is the most common.

Page 55 – The long u is presented here in the V-C-e pattern. The two sounds of u are the voice's natural response to the consonant before the u. The words in Section 3 can be read with either sound. Respond only with (u).

Add u-C-e as regular for spelling (u). Do not add u as the spelling response for (oo).

Page 56 – Add e-C-e for reading. There are few one-syllable words of this pattern. Chart e-C-e as the regular spelling of (e) in multisyllable words.

Page 57 — Add the -are family of words. The long sound of a is here altered some-what by the r sound and is frequently given another diacritical marking, but a long a sound is easier to explain to the student. The -are is the most common spelling for (ar) even though there is not a card response for it.

Add the Learned Words for, have, and what for both reading and spelling.

Page 58 — Add the (s) sound for c for reading, used when the c is before an e, i, or y. There are very few exceptions to this pattern; soccer is the most common. Once again the student is taught to see the letter clue that cues the correct sound. The nonsense syllables are common syllables from longer words which have the c (s).

Do not dictate these words or add c as a regular response for spelling (s). C (s) words must be memorized for spelling at the basic level.

LEVEL IIc – V-C-e words in compounds, with suffixes added, and in VC/CV patterns

Page 59 — Common compound words in which one of the words has the V-C-e pattern. Section #4 words are hyphenated. Students should follow spelling rules and generalizations already learned for any component word.

Page 60 — V-C-e words to which an ed suffix has been added.

Teach the spelling rule for dropping the silent e before a suffix beginning with a vowel if not already taught. Remember that d is not a suffix. The e is dropped and the ed suffix is added here.

The ed (ĕd) words in the right column are two-syllable words because of the t and d ending on the base word. Technically these are the V/CV pattern of LEVEL V, but it is more logical to include them here and focus on the base word. Do not teach the V/CV pattern now but remind the students of the (ĕd) after t or d.

Page 61 — These are V-C-e words with a consonant suffix added, which does not alter the base word spelling. Practice with these common suffixes is help-ful; -ful is pronounced like the word full, which is irregular; point this out.

The VC/CV or VCCCV words have a final V-C-e syllable which is usually accented because of the long sound. Advanced practice is in the *Angling Study Book*, pp. 65-87.

Page 62 — Add the Learned Words one, they, or, and where for reading and spelling. The practice includes c (s) words, so do not dictate those or sentences 1, 2, or 7.

LEVEL IId – Long single vowels in kind-old words, igh and the y-C-e pattern.

Page 63 — Add the word families where i and o are long even though the vowels are closed by two consonants. There should be sufficient practice to ensure that the students recognize these exceptions to the closed short vowel pat-tern. There are no *Phono-Cards* for these.

Page 64   –   Add the y-C-e pattern, remembering that y is a spelling for i, which gives the y the long i sound in this pattern. This page is not regular for spelling.

                Add igh (ī), which is regular for reading but not for spelling. The gh is an Old English spelling.

LEVEL IIIa –   Vowel digraphs in one-syllable words

Page 65   –   A vowel digraph is a combination of two vowels with one sound in one syllable. Often that sound is long, the sound of the name of the first vowel.

                Add ee (ē), a very common digraph regular for reading. It is also regular for spelling (ē) within a word and at the end of a word. All of the words on this page may be dictated for spelling except those ending in ze. Chart ee in the third space following (ē) on the chart.

                Additional advanced practice for the digraphs introduced through page 73 will be found in the *Angling for Words Study Book*, pages 162-177. T.L., pp. 86-89, has background material for both practice books.

Page 66   –   Introduce ea (ē), regular for reading but not for spelling. Do not dictate these words as regular.

Page 67   –   Mixed practice for discrimination between short vowels from LEVEL I and similar words with long digraphs. Do not dictate any ea words or sentences 4 - 11.

Page 68   –   Add oo (o͞o), the most common and regular long sound for oo. It is regular also for spelling, but refer to page 55 to review that long u also has this sound after consonants like l, r, t, and s, so u would be a possible spelling for (o͞o) in that position. Do not dictate section 5 or the sentences. A final (v) is always spelled ve, but a final (z) could be spelled either s or z as seen here. A silent e usually follows s or z.

Page 69   –   Add the short sound of oo (o͝o), as in book. It is a regular pronunciation in common words, regular for spelling. Words in sections #3 and #4 can have either pronunciation. Sentences 1-5 can be dictated.

Page 70   –   Add ai (ā), regular for reading but not for spelling. Add do, two, and who for reading and spelling.

Page 71   –   Mixed practice to assure discrimination and mastery. Dictate only the words regular for spelling.

Page 72   –   Add ay (ā), regular for reading and the regular spelling for (ā) at the end of a word. Review that y is a spelling for i and is the regular spelling at the end of a word; hence ai is always found within a word, and ay is the spelling at the end. The ay words may be dictated, as well as sentences 6 and 8.

Page 73   –   Add oa (ō), regular for reading but not for spelling.

Page 74 — Add oe (ō) and ow (ō). The (ō) pronunciation of ow is not as common as the cow (ou) to be introduced next, but these are fairly common words. For spelling, ow is the regular spelling for a final (ō) sound. The oe is regular for reading but not for spelling. Only sentence 3 should be dictated.

Page 75-76 — The ou (ou) and ow (ou) are properly labeled as *dipthongs,* not digraphs. A dipthong is a blend of two vowel sounds in one syllable. There are a number of pronunciations for ou in English, but (ou) is the most common and should always be tried first. The ow spelling is regular for (ou) at the end of a word, while ou is at the beginning or in the middle. All of page 75 may be dictated except ounce and sentences 3 and 6.

Add the Learned Words want, four, give, and were for both reading and spelling. The -own and -owl words are not regular for spelling, so the sentences should not be dictated.

Page 77-78 — The au and aw spellings for (au) are similar to ou-ow. They are all regular for reading; in spelling, au is regular within a word and aw at the end. Do not dictate section #2 on page 77; sentences 2, 4, 5, and 7 may be used. The al (aul) pronunciation and spelling are regular in one-syllable words, with the l doubled on the end. Check any of the mixed section words before dictating, and only sentence 2 should be used.

Page 79 — Add oy and oi, both (oi) and labeled dipthongs. They are regular for reading and spelling, oy being regular at the end of a word. Words may be dictated through section #2 except voice and choice (because of the ce.) Sentences 1, 2, and 5 may be used.

LEVEL IIIb – Two-syllable words with vowel digraphs

Pages 80-82 – These pages feature vowel digraphs with various suffixes added. On page 80, sections #1 and #3 may be dictated. Section #3 and sentences 1 and 2 on page 81 are also regular. Remind students to first spell the base word and then the suffix. On page 82, section #3 is regular for dictation, as are sentences 1, 2, and 3.

Pages 83-85 – These compound words are regular for reading, but do not dictate any words containing an ea or ai on page 83. The spelling rules for words continue to function in compounds.

On page 84 use only carefully selected regular words and sentences 2, 4, and 5 for spelling. All the practice words on page 85 may be dictated. Add the Learned Words for both reading and spelling: some, put, know, and any. Sentences 1, 6, 7, and 9 may be dictated.

Page 86 — Practice here is in dividing two syllable words between the middle consonants when one syllable contains a vowel digraph. Do not dictate ea or ai words, and only sentences 1, 2, and 3 are regular.

Page 87 — Continue practice with VC/CV words and digraphs. Words in section #1 may be dictated; remind students that a vowel before a double r is short. Therefore, when they hear a short vowel before r, the r is usually doubled.

Select dictation words carefully for regularity. Add for reading and spelling the Learned Words <u>been</u>, <u>very</u>, <u>about</u>, and <u>work</u>. Sentences 1, 3, 4, and 5 may be dictated.

Page 88 — In #1 and #2, the words are divided after the vowel digraph or dipthong. It is advisable not to use these words or sentences for spelling since many of them are irregular. Some of the compounds are regular.

LEVEL IVa – Vowel-<u>r</u> words

Page 89 — Add <u>er</u> (ẽr) in monosyllables and endings as well as suffixes seen previously on page 35. It will be seen that each of the vowel-<u>r</u> combinations can be pronounced (er), but only <u>er</u> is considered regular for spelling

Words in sections #2, #3, and #4 are the double consonant <u>rabbit</u> words introduced on page 42 or 1-1-1 rule words. These and sentences 1, 2, and 3 may be dictated.

Pages 90-91 — These pages have <u>er</u> words in which the <u>er</u> is not a suffix. On page 90 all words are regular for spelling except those with <u>c</u> before <u>e</u> and <u>i</u>. Sentences 1, 2, 4, and 5 may be dictated after the Learned Words <u>away</u>, <u>many</u>, <u>your</u>, and <u>other</u> are added. Check words on page 91 to be dictated since many are irregular.

Page 92 — Add <u>ur</u> (ûr), regular for reading but not for spelling.

Page 93 — Introduce <u>ir</u> (ûr), also regular for reading but not for spelling. <u>Squirrel</u> and <u>stirrup</u> are exceptions to the generalization on page 47 that a vowel before two <u>r</u>'s is pronounced short.

Page 94 — Add <u>ar</u> (ä), regular for reading in accented syllables and for spelling (ä). All of the words may be dictated. Add the Learned Words <u>could</u>, <u>would</u>, <u>don't</u>, and <u>again</u>. Do not dictate <u>nice</u> in sentence 4.

Page 95 — Two-syllable words with <u>ar</u> in the accented syllable are fairly common, as may be seen here. Sentences 3 and 5 are regular for dictation.

Page 96 — Add <u>or</u> (ôr), regular for reading in accented syllables and regular for spelling. Words in sections #1, #2, and #3 may be used for spelling except for <u>force</u>. The sentences, however, should not be used for spelling.

LEVEL IVb – Final unaccented vowel-<u>r</u> (ẽr) and multisyllable words with V<u>r</u>

Page 97 — In a final unaccented syllable, <u>ar</u> and <u>or</u> are each pronounced (ẽr). The spelling must be memorized. Call attention to the <u>sci</u> in <u>scissors</u>; since the <u>c</u> has the (s) sound before <u>i</u>, it is pronounced only once.

Page 98 — These three-syllable words each have a vowel-<u>r</u> syllable. Take care to check words for regularity for spelling before dictating. Only sentence 5 is regular.

LEVEL IVc – The consonant g (j) before <u>e</u>, <u>i</u>, or <u>y</u>

Page 99 — In section #1 are listed the most common words in which g retains its regular (g) sound before <u>e</u>, <u>i</u>, or <u>y</u>. However, g usually has the (j) sound before these vowels. The most common use of g̲e̲ is for the final (j) sound since English does not end words with a j̲. It is regular to spell (j) with a g before e̲, i̲, or y̲ except in the root syllable j̲e̲c̲t̲. Note that in the -nge words in section #3, the two consonants keep the vowel short. Sentence 1 may be dictated. More advanced practice for g (j) is in the *Angling for Words Study Book*, pages 115-116, and in the *Workbook* page 39.

Page 100 – On this page are several groups of words with g̲e̲. The final syllable -a̲g̲e̲ is pronounced (ĭj). In section #4, the final e̲s̲ must be pronounced as a separate syllable after g because it is too difficult to say or to hear the (s) after (j). If a student has difficulty with these words, advise him to focus on the base word without the s̲ and then add (ĕz). The family of a̲n̲g̲e̲ words are similar to the k̲i̲n̲d̲-o̲l̲d̲ words on page 63. Words with u̲r̲ on this page should not be dictated.

LEVEL V – Open vowel/consonant-vowel words V/CV

Pages 101-3 – The words on these pages are of the open, long vowel/consonant vowel pattern, (V̄/CV), the first vowel being long because it is at the end of an accented syllable. The sections contain identical words on the two pages but in a mixed order; the words on 101 are separated at the syllable division to aid students in seeing the break. Note that in a Vr̲V word, the vowel-r̲ does not have the special sounds of Level IV. The r̲ acts as any other consonant. Review the open vowels on page 49.

Page 102 lists the same words in a different order and without the space at the division. If there is still difficulty evident in dividing the syllables visually, page 102 may be copied and the division marked with a vertical line by the student.

The regular spelling for a long vowel sound at the end of an accented syllable is the single named vowel. These words are regular for spelling if the vowel sound in the second syllable can be heard. Pronounce the unaccented syllables as accented when dictating. Sentences 2 on page 101 and 1, 3, 5, and 6 on 102 may be dictated. Words on page 103 are mixed and many are regular; the sentences contain irregularities in spelling. Note the common adjective ending, -a̲l̲, on words in section 3.

Page 104 – Here the -b̲l̲e̲ type syllable of page 38 is combined with an open, accented, long vowel syllable. Exercises for discrimination between the closed, short first syllable and the open, long one are found in sections #2 and #3. These words are all regular for dictation, as are the sentences after the Learned Words (p̲u̲l̲l̲, f̲u̲l̲l̲, o̲n̲l̲y̲, and l̲i̲v̲e̲) are mastered.

Page 105 – In these words a vowel suffix has been added to a base word, causing a spelling change. Section #1 has vowel-consonant-e̲ words where the silent e̲ was dropped when the vowel suffix was added. This change causes the syllable division to be after the first vowel, making it open, accented, and long. In sections #2 and #3 this pattern is contrasted for reading with words where the final consonant of a base word with a single short vowel has been doubled when a vowel suffix was added. If these rules have been taught, these words are good for dictation. Sentences 1 and 3 are regular.

Pages 106-107 – In the words on these pages, the accent falls on the second syllable, and the first vowel is open and unaccented. The open e, o, and u on pages 106 and 107 have a "half-long" pronunciation. Since the vowel in an accented syllable is usually regular phonetically, words on 106 and 107 may be dictated for spelling. Sentences 1 and 2 on page 106 and 2 on 107 may be dictated. Learn today, buy, once, and pretty.

Page 108 – On page 108, the open unaccented vowel is an a, which has the obscure or schwa sound (ə) or (ŭ). At the end of a word or unaccented syllable, (ŭ) is regularly spelled a. All of the words and sentences on this page may be dictated except afraid and aboard.

Page 109 – As seen on page 109, an open unaccented i is regularly short. Sections #2 and #3 demonstrate how common the unaccented i is in the middle syllable. Students can spell most of these words easily if they are pronounced and spelled by syllables. Sentences 1 and 3 may be dictated. Many of these words and those on the remaining pages are from lists of essential vocabulary for adults and may be omitted for younger students if desired.

Page 110 – Most of these multisyllables can now be spelled, but words containing ea, oa, c(s), and long y are irregular. Sentences 2 and 3 may be dictated.

LEVEL VI – Assorted digraphs, patterns, and word groups

Pages 111-112 – These pages feature the most common silent consonant combinations: initial kn and wr on 111, final mb, and medial t and l on 112. Obviously, these spellings must be memorized.

Page 113 – Add dge (j), regularly found immediately after a short vowel. This is the regular spelling for (j) at the end of a one-syllable word after a short vowel. This page is regular for spelling. Advanced practice on the (j) spelling is in the *Angling Workbook*, pages 38-42.

Page 114-115 – On these two pages are some of the common words of the VCV pattern where the syllable division falls after the consonant, making the first vowel short. The first two sections have the syllable division shown. This pattern and these pages are irregular for spelling. In section #2 the consonant digraphs close the first vowel, acting as a single consonant. The three syllable words in section #3 on page 115 are additional essential functional words.

Page 116 – Add the short (ĕ) sound of ea found predominately in everyday words from the Anglo-Saxon language. The ea (ĕ) words must be memorized for spelling, so do not dictate. The s in measure, treasure, and pleasure is (zh), which the voice will make naturally before long u.

Page 117 – Add the (ŭ) sound of o, found in common words, usually before an n, m, v, or th. It is not regular for spelling. Add does, blue, their, and laugh.

Page 118 — On this page are listed three phonograms found in fairly common small groups: <u>wa</u> (wŏ), <u>ey</u> (ē), and <u>ew</u> (ū). The <u>wa</u> is regular for spelling; <u>ey</u> and <u>ew</u> are not.

Page 119 — Add the common -<u>tion</u> (shŭn) noun suffix, considered regular for reading and spelling. Always accent the syllable just before the -<u>tion</u>. An <u>i</u> before -<u>tion</u> remains short, even though accented. All the words listed and sentences 2-5 may be dictated for spelling.

NOTE: Some common spelling rules are not covered in this book. To complete the spelling program on the basic level, cover all plural rules and the final <u>y</u> rule. See <u>T.L.</u>, pp. 109-120.

APPENDIX

Basic Angling Phonetic Skills Survey

Permission is granted to reproduce the record sheets for this survey test. Each student to be individually tested requires a separate copy of the record sheets.

To administer the survey:

1. The student uses the lists found on the first two pages of the *Practice Book*. Instruct him to read each nonsense word on the lists slowly and distinctly.

   For students uncomfortable with nonsense words, explain that each *could* be a real word and is often part of a real word. Encourage the student to try each word since his response tells you what type of mistakes he makes.

2. The levels on the test match the levels of instruction in the book, and the nonsense words include all important phonograms or patterns to be mastered in each list.

   If desired, the individual levels can be given as pre-tests (and later as post-tests) instead of the entire test being administered at one sitting.

3. If the student pronounces the word correctly, place a check on the line *before* the number. If there is an error in any phonogram, write the phonetic spelling of that response in the space for its location in the word.

   HEADINGS KEY: C – consonant; V – vowel; CC – consonant blend; CD – consonant digraph (two or more consonants making one sound); and VC – vowel digraph (two or more vowels making one sound.)

4. It is best to place the recording sheet so that the student cannot watch the marking.

5. Errors made on the test will clearly display which levels or phonograms the student has mastered and which he has particular difficulty with. These weaknesses can indicate how difficult the remediation may be and which levels will need special attention.

6. The survey record sheet may be reused as a post-test record by using a different color of marking ink. Be sure to date each administration in the ink color.

KEY to the *Phonetic Skills Survey* using similar *real* words:

Ia	u<u>ni</u>t	II	he	IVa	samp<u>ler</u>
	gas		sly		stir
	step		babe		stir
	<u>hom</u>iny		bike		roar
	cud		loaf		star
	rib		im<u>mune</u>		
	wet + Jeff		meet	IVc	<u>gon</u>dola
	tax		type		jet or get
	yam + bog		care		page
	just + buzz		lose or loose		
				V	no
			set		see
			cat + rag		few
Ib	drop		Sid		
	<u>gl</u>itter		cot + loss or Oz		
	smut		sill		
	brad		mild		navel or ravel
	held		bold		by/pan or nip/an
	<u>hist</u>ory		my		few/lit or dull/it
	stomp				no/ble
	neck	III	sleet		say/puh
	<u>trun</u>k		bean		
	<u>jan</u>gle		spoof or book		
			gape	VI	badge
	shun		<u>za</u>´ny		<u>wa</u>ter
	<u>th</u>ank or <u>th</u>an		toad		new
	chin + jog		toe		nation
	whip		fowl		
	Beth		how or slow		
	hutch		raw		
	quit		dawn		
			hall		
Ic	<u>hemp</u> (ĭng)		boy		
	<u>off</u> - (ĭ) or (ĕ)		coil		
	badly				
	pitted (ĕd)				
	supped (t)				
	planter				
	beds				
	boxes				
	spindle				
	gas/ or has/pet				
	spud/sip				
	sling/lit				
	<u>wear</u>-in				

Note: When alternative pronunciations are acceptable, both are given with the word <u>or</u>. Mark which is chosen by the student.

Basic Angling Phonetic Skills Survey

Name_____ Grade_____ Date_____

LEVEL Ia	C	V	C
____ nit	_____	_____	_____
____ las	_____	_____	_____
____ fep	_____	_____	_____
____ hom	_____	_____	_____
____ kud	_____	_____	_____
____ vib	_____	_____	_____
____ weff	_____	_____	_____
____ cax	_____	_____	_____
____ yog	_____	_____	_____
____ juz	_____	_____	_____

LEVEL Ib	CC	V	CC
____ dron	_____	_____	_____
____ glit	_____	_____	_____
____ smup	_____	_____	_____
____ crad	_____	_____	_____
____ beld	_____	_____	_____
____ hist	_____	_____	_____
____ fomp	_____	_____	_____
____ keck	_____	_____	_____
____ runk	_____	_____	_____
____ jang	_____	_____	_____

LEVEL Ib	CD	V	CD
____ shum	_____	_____	_____
____ thap	_____	_____	_____
____ chog	_____	_____	_____
____ whib	_____	_____	_____
____ heth	_____	_____	_____
____ rutch	_____	_____	_____
____ quid	_____	_____	_____

LEVEL Ic	C V C / Suffix or CVC
____ semp/ing	_____ / _____
____ dof/fy	_____ / _____
____ cad/ly	_____ / _____
____ bit/ted	_____ / _____
____ gupped	_____
____ lan/ter	_____ / _____
____ med's	_____
____ hoxes	_____ / _____
____ pin/dle	_____ / _____
____ ras/pet	_____ / _____
____ grud/sip	_____ / _____
____ pling/lit	_____ / _____
____ fer/rin	_____ / _____

Basic Angling Phonetic Skills Survey (Cont.)

Name_____ Grade_____ Date_____

LEVEL IIc	C	V	C
___ nit	__	__	
___ bly	__	__	
___ habe	__	__	__
___ vike	__	__	__
___ rofe	__	__	__
___ mune	__	__	__
___ dete	__	__	__
___ sype	__	__	__
___ nare	__	__	__
___ luse	__	__	__

	C	V	C
___ cet	__	__	__
___ cag	__	__	
___ cid	__	__	__
___ cos	__	__	__
___ cyl	__	__	__
___ hiled	__	__	__
___ pold	__	__	__
___ kigh	__	__	__

LEVEL III	C	VD	C
___ leet	__	__	__
___ vean	__	__	__
___ boof	__	__	__
___ gaip	__	__	__
___ zay	__	__	
___ noad	__	__	__
___ soe	__	__	
___ roul	__	__	
___ pow	__	__	__
___ daw	__	__	
___ taun	__	__	__
___ jall	__	__	__
___ hoy	__	__	
___ coip	__	__	__

LEVEL IV	CC	V
___ pler	__	__
___ stur	__	__
___ smir	__	__
___ tror	__	__
___ clar	__	__

LEVEL IVc	C	V	C
___ gon	__	__	__
___ gep	__	__	__
___ lage	__	__	__

LEVEL V	C	V
___ bo´	__	__
___ re´	__	__
___ fu´	__	__
___ savel	_____	
___ nipan	_____	
___ pulit	_____	
___ joble	_____	
___ tapa	_____	

LEVEL VI	C	V	C
___ fadge	__	__	__
___ wam	__	__	__
___ kew	__	__	__
___ lation	_____		

NOTES:

Suggested Lesson Plan Order

Date:_____ Student or Class:_____

   I. READING

      A. *Phono-Card* deck responses

      B. Review of recent phonograms; *Basic Angling* pages:

      C. Add card: Page: #

      D. Supplemental practice: Book:

          Pages:

  II. SPELLING

      A. *Phono-Card* spelling responses

      B. Dictation: *Basic Angling* pages:

          Words:

Sample Lesson

   I. A. *Phono-Card* responses

      B. Review short <u>e</u>, p. 7: #3 vertically; #4; #6 nonsense; p. 8 #1 vertical; #4 across

      C. Add <u>w</u> p. 8 #5

         Add Learned Words on cards: <u>the</u>, <u>go</u>, <u>he</u>, <u>of</u>, <u>to</u>

         Sentences: p. 9, #1-7

  II. A. Spelling responses – write

      B. Review <u>ff</u>, <u>ll</u>, <u>ss</u> generalization; add <u>w</u>;

      C. Dictation:

         1. will 2. wet 3. well 4. wig 5. web 6. win

            pet wags   big win   will wed   run well

         Sent. #1, 2 p. 9

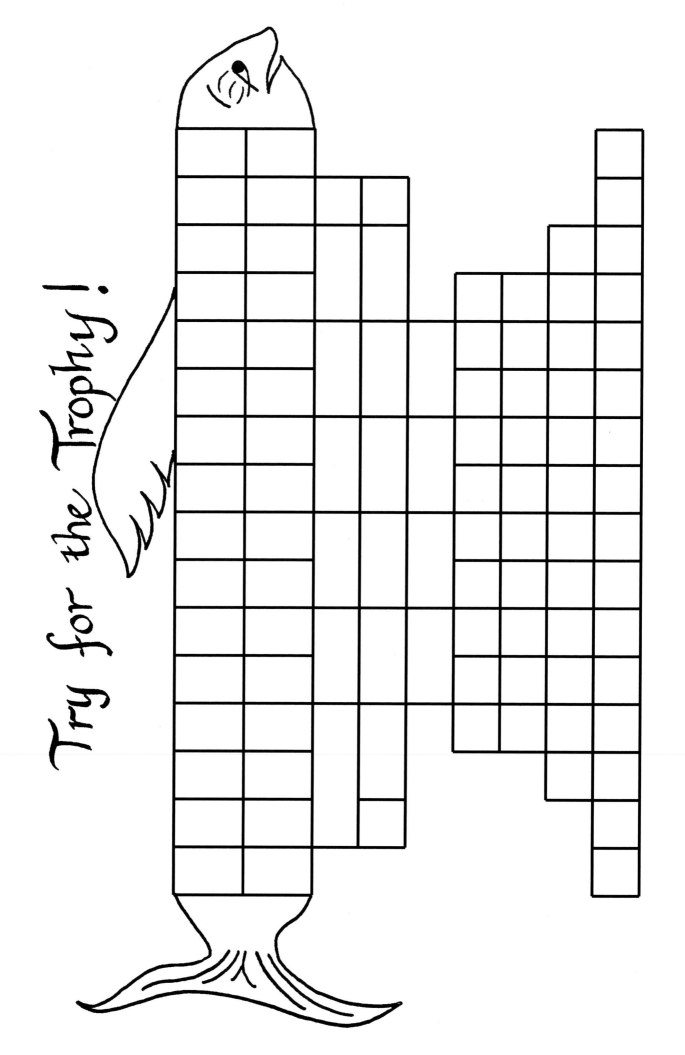

Try for the Trophy!

Try for the Trophy!

KEY

A phonics skills review chart (fish-shaped). Level labels and cell contents as follows:

LEVEL IV	er · ur · ir · ar · or · Final / ar-or · (j) / g · V'/CV V/CV' · à · silent · dge · VC/V · ĕā · (ŭ) / o · tion
LEVEL V	ee · ēā · ŏŏ · ŏŏ · ai · ay · oa · oe · ōw · ow (ou) · aw (ou) · au (aul) · al · oy · oi
LEVEL VI	—
LEVEL IId	—
LEVEL III	V̄' · V - C - ¢ Compounds · V - C - ¢ + ed · V - C - ¢ + cons. s · V'/CV V/CV' · VC/CVC-¢ · VC/CV-¢ · kind-old · y - C - ¢ · igh
LEVEL IIc	- āre · (s) c
LEVEL IIb	a - ¢ · i - ¢ · o - ¢ · u - ¢ · e - ¢ · V̆ r̲ r̲ V · V̆ r̲ V
LEVEL Ic	Compounds · -ing · -ŷ · -ly · -ĕd · -ed (t) · -ed (d) · -er · -es · 's · -C<u>le</u>
LEVEL Ic	ck · nk · ng · -s · sh · th · ƫ · ch · tch · wh · qu
LEVEL Ib	ă · ĭ · (z) ş · ŭ · ff · ĕ · (g) y · con. y · r · w · ð · ð (k) c
LEVEL Ia	t · p · n · (s) s · d · l · f · h · g · m · r · (k) c · k · b · j · v · x · z · c

Basic Angling
Spelling Curriculum and Reference

Phonogram Sequence	Student Book page	Teacher's Manual page	Teacher's Line page	Learned Words
(t) t, (p) p, (n) n,	1	T 6	36	a
(s) s, (l) l, (d) d	1	T 6	36, 37	
(f) f, (h) h, (g) g,	1	T 6	38	
(m) m, (r) r, (k) c,	1	T 6	40, 45	
(k) k, (b) b, (j) j,	1	T 6	45, 48	
(v) v	1	T 6	52	

The phonograms above and a are assumed mastered for both reading and spelling before entry into the *Basic Angling Practice Book*.

LEVEL Ia – Short Vowels and Single Consonant Sounds:

(ă) a	1	T 8	37	
Initial (k) c;	1	T 9	45	
k before e,	2	T 9	45	
i, or y				
(ĭ) i	2	T 11	36	
Final (z) s	4	T 11	36	
(ŭ) u	5	T 12	44	Exceptions:
Final ff, ll, ss	6	T 12	38	if, us, bus
(ĕ) e	7	T 12	40	yes, gas, pal
(w) w	8	T 12	51	
(y) y	9	T 12	42	the, he,
(ŏ) o	10	T 12	39	go, of, to
(ks) x	11	T 12	53	
(z) 2nd resp. z	11	T 12	52	I, you

LEVEL Ib – Short Vowels and Consonant Blends:

Final (k) after				
consonant: k	14	T 13	46	
(ă) a + blends	14	T 13	37	
(ĭ) i + blends	15	T 13	36, 45	
(ŭ) u + blends	16	T 13	44	
(ĕ) e + blends	18	T 13	40	
(ŏ) o + blends	19	T 13	39	
Generalization:				
Final (k) right after				there
short vowel – ck	23	T 13	47	come, are
(ngk) nk	24	T 13	46	
(ng) ng	24	T 13	38	
(sh) sh	25	T 13	71	
(th), (th̶) th	26	T 13	73	this, thus
(ch) ch	27	T 13	71	

Spelling Curriculum (cont.)

Phonogram Sequence	Student Book page	Teacher's Manual page	Teacher's Line page	Learned Words
Generalization:				Exceptions:
(ch) t<u>ch</u> right	27	T 13	72	<u>such</u>, <u>much</u>,
after short vowel				<u>rich</u>
(hw) <u>wh</u>	28	T 13	74	<u>which</u>
(kw) <u>qu</u>	28	T 13	53, 54	
LEVEL Ic – Short Vowels, Suffixes, Compound Words, VC/CV:				
(ĭng) -<u>ing</u>	29	T 14	39	
[Doubling 1-1-1				
rule optional]	29	T 14	[111]	
(ĭ) 2nd resp. <u>y</u>	30	T 14	43	
(lĭ) – <u>ly</u>	31	T 14	51	<u>Mr.</u>, <u>Mrs.</u>,
				<u>said</u>
(ĕd) -<u>ed</u>; [1-1-1]	32	T 14	51	
(t) 2nd resp. <u>ed</u>	33	T 14	50	
(d) 2nd resp. <u>ed</u>	34	T 14	50	
(ẽr) -<u>er</u> suffix	35	T 15	65	
Contractions or				<u>here</u>, <u>look</u>,
possessives	36	T 15	116	<u>was</u>
(ĕz) -<u>es</u> after	37	T 15	75	
<u>s</u>, <u>x</u>, <u>z</u>, <u>ch</u>, <u>sh</u>				
-Consonant <u>le</u>	38	T 15	100	
-Cons. <u>le</u> + <u>ed</u>				
[optional here]	39	T 15	[110]	
Compound words	40	T 15		
VC´/CV	42	T 15	42	
"rabbit" VC/CV	42	T 15	54	
VC/C<u>y</u>	45	T 15	43, [111]	
VCCCV	47	T 16	42	
V̆<u>r</u>/<u>r</u>V	47	T 16	41	
LEVEL IIa – Open Long Vowels				
One-syllable final				
(ā) <u>a</u>, (ē) <u>e</u>,	49	T 16		
(ī) <u>i</u>, (ō) <u>o</u>	49	T 16	49	
(ī) <u>y</u>	49	T 16	43	
LEVEL IIb – Vowel Consonant-Silent <u>e</u>				
(ā) <u>a</u>-C-<u>e</u>	50	T 16	59	
(ĭ) <u>i</u>-C-<u>e</u>	52	T 16	59	
(ō) <u>o</u>-C-<u>e</u>	53	T 16	59	
(ū) <u>u</u>-C-<u>e</u>	55	T 16	59	
(ē) <u>e</u>-C-<u>e</u>	56	T 16	59	
(ā) -<u>are</u>	57	T 17	57	<u>for</u>, <u>have</u>, <u>what</u>

Spelling Curriculum (cont.)

Phonogram Sequence	Student Book page	Teacher's Edition page	Teacher's Line page	Learned Words
LEVEL IIc – V-C-e Two-syllable Words				
V-C-e + suffix	60, 61	T 17	61, 110	one, they, or, where
LEVEL IIIa – Vowel Digraphs				
(ē) medial, final ee	65	T 18	86	
(ōō) oo	68	T 18	87	
(ŏŏ) oo	69	T 18	88	do, two, who
(ā) at end ay	72	T 18	89	
(ō) at end ow	74	T 19	91	
(ou) ou	75	T 19	90	
(ou) at end ow	76	T 19	90	want, four,
(au) at end aw	77	T 19	91	give, were
(au) au	77	T 19	91	
(aul) al	78	T 19	98	
(oi) at end oy	79	T 19	92	
(oi) oi	79	T 19	92	some, put, know, any been, very, about, work
LEVEL IVa – Vowel - r				
(ẽr) er	89 90	T 20	65	away, many, your, other
(är) ar	94	T 20	67	could, would, don't, again
(ô) or	96	T 20	66	
LEVEL IVc – g (j)				
(j) g before e, i or y usually	99	T 20	69	
(ĭj) -age	100	T 21	70	
LEVEL V – Open Vowels in Multisyllables				
V̄´CV – a, e, i, o, u	101	T 21	78	
V̄´Cle	104	T 21	100	pull, full, only, live
(ŭ) unaccented open a	108	T 22	82	today, buy, once, pretty
LEVEL VI – Assorted Phonograms				
(j) dge right after short vowel	113	T 22	69	
(wŏ) wa	118	T 23	52	does, blue
(shŭn) -tion	119	T 23	103	their, laugh

T 34

Name: _____

Spelling Chart – Regular Spellings Covered

(t) ___ ; ___   (ă) ___   (hw) ___

(p) ___   (ĭ) ___ ; ___   (kw) ___

(n) ___   (z) ___ ; ___   (b´l) ___

(s) ___   (ŭ) ___ ; ___   (ā) ___ ; ___ ; ___

(l) ___   (ĕ) ___   (ī) ___ ; ___ ; ___

(d) ___ ; ___   (w) ___   (ō) ___ ; ___ ; ___

(f) ___   (y) ___   (ū) ___ ; ___

(h) ___   (ŏ) ___   (ē) ___ ; ___ ; ___

(g) ___   (wŏ) ___   (o͞o) ___

(m) ___   (ks) ___   (o͝o) ___

(r) ___   (ngk) ___   (ou) ___ ; ___

(k) ___ ; ___ ; ___   (ng) ___   (au) ___ ; ___ ; ___

(b) ___   (sh) ___   (oi) ___ ; ___

(j) ___ ; ___ ; ___   (th) ___   (ĕr) ___

(v) ___   (t̶h̶) ___   (är) ___

                      (ch) ___ ; ___   (ôr) ___

                                        (shŭn) ___

Rules and Generalizations

Date covered:

(k) Initial _____

    Final _____

(f), (l), (s) doubling _____

(ch) _____

Doubling medial consonant _____

1-1-1 doubling _____

Final e + suffix _____

(j) _____

y rules _____

Plural rules _____

Name: _____

Spelling Chart – Regular Spellings Covered

(t)	t; -ed	(ă)	a	(hw)	wh
(p)	p	(ĭ)	i; y	(kw)	qu
(n)	n	(z)	s; z	(b´l)	ble
(s)	s	(ŭ)	u; a	(ā)	a; a-e; ay
(l)	l	(ě)	e	(ĭ)	i; i-e; y
(d)	d; ed	(w)	w	(ō)	o; o-e; ow
(f)	f	(y)	y	(ū)	u; u-e
(h)	h	(ŏ)	o	(ē)	e; e-e; ee
(g)	g	(wŏ)	wa	(o͞o)	oo
(m)	m	(ks)	x	(o͝o)	oo
(r)	r	(ngk)	nk	(ou)	ou; ow
(k)	c; k; ck	(ng)	ng	(au)	au; aw; al
(b)	b	(sh)	sh	(oi)	oi; oy
(j)	j; g; dge	(th)	th	(ẽr)	er
(v)	v	(t̶h̶)	th	(är)	ar
		(ch)	ch; tch	(ôr)	or
				(shŭn)	tion

Rules and Generalizations

Date covered:

(k) Initial _____

    Final _____

(f), (l), (s) doubling_____

(ch) _____

Doubling medial consonant _____

1-1-1 doubling _____

Final e + suffix_____

(j)_____

y rules_____

Plural rules_____

Supplementary Practice Word Lists

Additional Functional Words – Regular for Reading
with *Basic Angling* Phonograms

application	attendant	authorized
available	bottom	budget
careful	chance	citizen
city	clearance	color
combustible	construction	contaminated
credit	dairy	department
dependent	deposit	disability
discount	distance	disturb
dozen	during	elevator
entrance	explosives	exceed
express	external	exit
gentlemen	husband	include
information	manager	minors
money	nickel	occupation
orange	per	personnel
program	prosecuted	property
quiet	resume	security
station	supply	system
Thanksgiving	traffic	United States
vacation	vegetable	voucher

Supplementary Practice Word Lists

The following words are functional words which are phonetically regular but contain phonograms not covered in *Basic Angling*. These phonograms or patterns are covered in the *Angling for Words Study Book*, which can be used for additional practice.

annual	area	auditorium
avenue	bear	believe
break	bruise	cafeteria
cashier	chemicals	cigarette
continue	cried	detour
freight	fruit	furniture
goes	great	group
individual	juice	ladies
married	material	mechanical
mountain	neighbor	noxious
pedestrian	period	picture
piece	poisonous	quality
quart	quarter	radio
school	signature	social
soup	special	steak
suit	tear	telephone
television	tried	union
violators	war	warm
warning	wear	weight
word	work	world
worse	worst	yield

Supplementary Practice Word Lists

The following functional words are not phonetically regular and must be memorized for reading and spelling:

against	although	altogether
answer	anyone	anything
anywhere	aunt	automobile
ballet	beautiful	beauty
blood	bloody	bought
brought	build	building
built	bury	bush
business	busy	caught
certain	certificate	Christ
Christmas	clothes	coming
country	couple	courage
course	courts	cousin
daughter	done	door
double	early	earn
earth	engine	enough
experience	extinguisher	eye
father	flood	floor
foreign	fourth	fragile
friend	garage	gasoline
gone	guard	guess
handkerchief	heard	heart

Irregular Functional Words (continued)

height	honest	hour
insurance	iron	island
John	knew	learn
liquor	lose	machine
medicine	minute	mortgage
move	movie	national
naughty	ocean	oh
opposite	ought	pear
people	police	prove
pull	push	question
real	really	residential
rough	safety	says
service	sew	shoe
should	shoulder	shove
sign	soldier	sometimes
sought	straight	sugar
sure	taught	though
thought	through	tomorrow
tonight	tongue	touch
tough	toward	view
voltage	Wednesday	whose
whole	wolf	woman
women	worry	young